THE WONDERFUL SWEAR WORD COLORING BOOK FOR ADULTS!

VOL. 1
MG PUBLICATION
© 2016. ALL RIGHTS RESERVED.

NO PART OF THIS BOOK MAY BE REPRODUCED IN ANY WRITTEN, ELECTRONIC, RECORDING, OR PHOTOCOPYING WITHOUT WRITTEN PERMISSION OF THE PUBLISHER OR AUTHOR.

PRINTED IN THE U.S.A.

THIS WONDERFUL BOOK
BELONGS TO

_____

QUOTES

"EVERYBODY LIKES A COMPLIMENT."
ABRAHAM LINCOLN

"WHEN IN DOUBT TELL THE TRUTH."
MARK TWAIN

"YOUR IN PRETTY GOOD SHAPE FOR THE SHAPE YOUR IN"
DR SUESS

"IT IS BETTER TO LIGHT A CANDLE THAN CURSE THE DARKNESS"
ELEANOR ROOSEVELT

"THIS BOOK CONTAINS A LOT OF 'BAD' WORDS. SO IF YOUR EASILY OFFENDED, GO FUCK YOURSELF."
OLIVER MARKUS

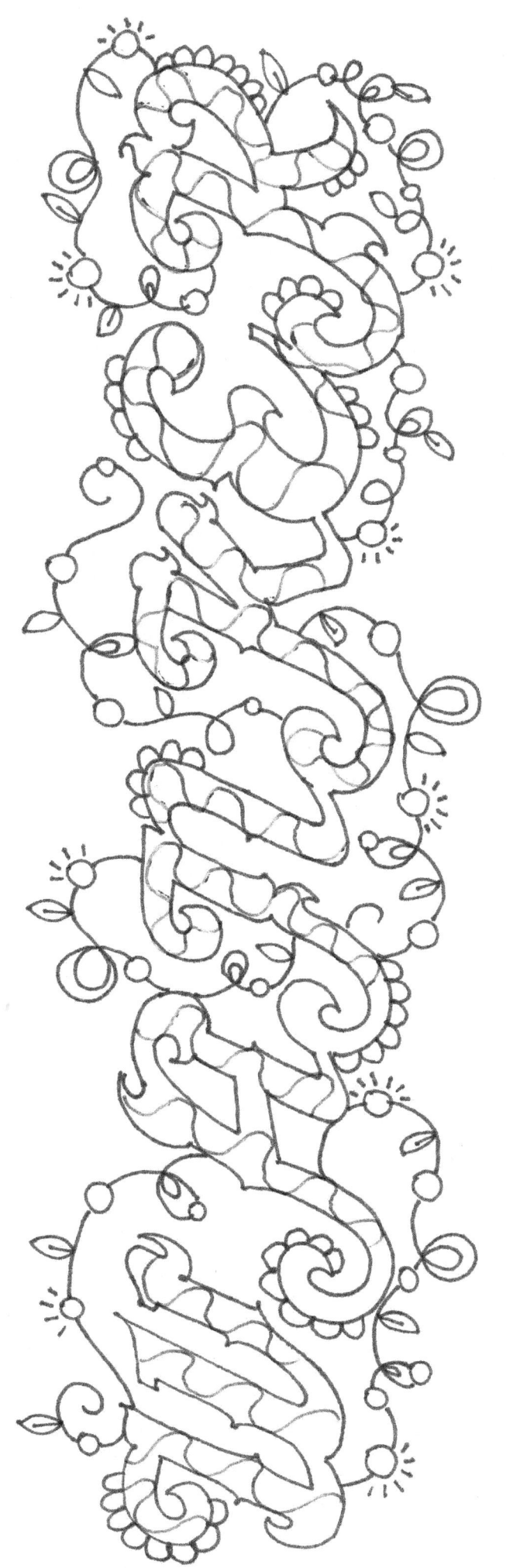

www.ingramcontent.com/pod-product-compliance
Lightning Source LLC
Chambersburg PA
CBHW081021040426
42444CB00014B/3302